THE USA

BY

SHALINI VALLEPUR

BookLife
PUBLISHING

©2019
BookLife Publishing Ltd.
King's Lynn
Norfolk PE30 4LS
All rights reserved.
Printed in Malaysia.

A catalogue record for this book is available from the British Library.

ISBN: 978-1-78637-689-3

Written by:
Shalini Vallepur

Edited by:
John Wood

Designed by:
Gareth Liddington

CONTENTS

Page 4   Welcome to the USA

Page 6   Houston Space Centre

Page 8   The French Quarter

Page 10   Everglades National Park

Page 12   Washington Monument

Page 14   The Statue of Liberty

Page 16   Lake Erie

Page 18   Millennium Park

Page 20   Mount Rushmore National Memorial

Page 22   Space Needle

Page 24   Golden Gate Bridge

Page 26   Mesa Verde National Park

Page 28   The Journey

Page 30   Goodbye

Page 31   Glossary

Page 32   Index

Words that look like this can be found in the glossary on page 31.

WELCOME TO THE USA

Hi! My name is Jacob. I live in Houston, Texas in the USA with my family. We are going on a big road trip around the USA. We want to see as much as we can.

Look out for coordinates in boxes like these. Use the internet to explore these places online. You can ask an adult to help you.

People have been living in the land that we now call the USA for over 15,000 years. Today, people from all around the world live in the USA. I can't wait to see all the different things in my country.

THERE ARE 50 STARS ON THE FLAG OF THE USA, ONE FOR EVERY STATE IN THE COUNTRY.

THE 50 STATES

USA stands for United States of America. There are 50 states that make up the USA. Each state has its own history and <u>culture</u>. A state is an area of land that has its own state <u>government</u>. States can make their own laws but there are laws made by the <u>federal</u> government that everyone in the USA must follow.

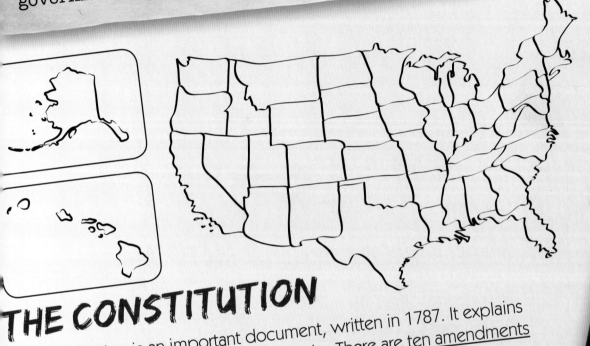

THE CONSTITUTION

The Constitution is an important document, written in 1787. It explains basic laws and how the government works. There are ten <u>amendments</u> that give citizens of the USA special rights.

HOUSTON SPACE CENTRE

Welcome to my hometown: Houston! My favourite place to visit is the space centre. We went to the space shuttle <u>exhibition</u>. There was a <u>replica</u> space shuttle sitting on top of a big plane.

WE WENT INSIDE THE SPACE SHUTTLE.

MISSION CONTROL

We saw the mission control room. Flight controllers use the computers in this room to talk to the astronauts who live and work in space on board the International Space Station.

THE JOURNEY BEGINS IN TEXAS

Houston Space Centre is in Texas. Texas is the second-biggest state in the USA, after Alaska. I love living in Texas because the weather is nice and hot. Sometimes there are tornadoes.

TEX-MEX

Tex-Mex is a <u>cuisine</u> from Texas. Texas is next to the country Mexico. People began to cook food from Mexico using ingredients from Texas. This led to a new type of food – Tex-Mex! Tex-Mex is popular all over the USA.

MY CHIMICHANGA HAD BEEF AND BEANS INSIDE IT.

THE FRENCH QUARTER

We reached the French Quarter in the city of New Orleans. The French Quarter was founded in the year 1718. I loved seeing all the buildings here. The <u>architecture</u> is a mix of French and Spanish styles.

A LOT OF BUILDINGS IN THE FRENCH QUARTER HAVE SPANISH BALCONIES.

NEW ORLEANS

New Orleans is in the state of Louisiana. The Mississippi River is the longest river in the USA and it runs through Louisiana. Lots of people came to New Orleans on boats that sailed along the Mississippi River.

THE STREETCAR WAS FUN TO RIDE!

MARDI GRAS

Mardi Gras is a big <u>carnival</u> that happens in New Orleans before the Christian season of Lent. The biggest celebrations in the USA are in New Orleans. There were big <u>floats</u> going down the street. Everybody was wearing costumes and masks. People on the floats were throwing beads into the crowd below – Dad caught loads!

'MARDI GRAS' IS FRENCH AND MEANS 'FAT TUESDAY' IN ENGLISH.

OYSTERS

WHAT IS CREOLE CUISINE?

There was a lot of Creole food on sale at Mardi Gras. Creole food is a mix of French, Spanish, African American and Native American cooking styles. We ate lots of different food around the French Quarter.

I ATE CREOLE OYSTERS. THEY HAD LOTS OF GARLIC.

EVERGLADES NATIONAL PARK

We made it to Everglades National Park in the state of Florida. The Everglades is a wetland. This means that there are areas of swampland and marshes.

AIRBOATS IN THE EVERGLADES

We took an airboat tour through the Everglades. Airboats are watercraft with a big fan on the back. The fan pushes the boat through the water. The waters in the Everglades are <u>shallow</u>, so airboats work best.

THE WATER LOOKED REALLY GREEN.

WE EXPLORED THE WATERWAYS OF THE EVERGLADES.

AMERICAN ALLIGATORS

American alligators are big <u>reptiles</u> that live in the Everglades. We saw an alligator when we went on the airboat tour. Alligators are very fast swimmers but the one we saw was resting.

ALLIGATOR

ALLIGATORS ARE A SYMBOL OF THE STATE OF FLORIDA.

FLORA AND FAUNA IN FLORIDA

Many interesting plants grow in Florida because it has a tropical and sub-tropical climate. This means there is a lot of rain and temperatures can get hot. We saw a manchineel tree. It is a poisonous tree that is very dangerous.

WASHINGTON MONUMENT

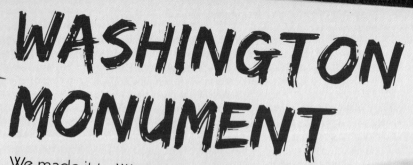

We made it to Washington DC, the capital city of the USA. There is so much to see! We visited the Washington Monument first. The Washington Monument was planned by Robert Mills. It is shaped like an Egyptian <u>obelisk</u>.

WASHINGTON MONUMENT COORDINATES
38.8894706, -77.0393257

THE MONUMENT WAS THE TALLEST STRUCTURE IN THE WORLD WHEN IT WAS BUILT.

The building began in 1848 and was finished in 1884. It took a long time because it was being made out of stone. It was built to remember George Washington.

WHO WAS GEORGE WASHINGTON?

George Washington was the first president of the USA. He led the army during the American Revolutionary War in the years 1775-1783. The Washington Monument remembers Washington and his good leadership.

GEORGE WASHINGTON IS KNOWN AS ONE OF THE 'FOUNDING FATHERS' OF THE USA.

THE WHITE HOUSE

The White House is close to the Washington Monument, so we saw it too. This is a big building where the president of the USA lives. George Washington chose where the house was built in 1791.

THE STATUE OF LIBERTY

Next stop: The Statue of Liberty. It is on Liberty Island in New York City. We had to take a ferry to get there. The statue is a <u>monument</u> that celebrates American <u>independence</u> and freedom.

MOM FELT SEASICK ON THE FERRY.

STATUE

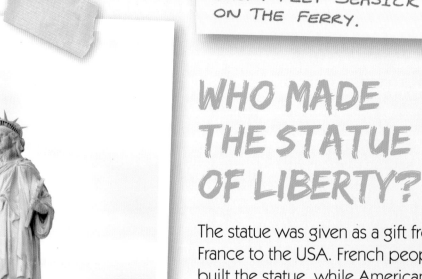

PEDESTAL

WHO MADE THE STATUE OF LIBERTY?

The statue was given as a gift from France to the USA. French people built the statue, while American people built the <u>pedestal</u> that it stands on. The statue is made of copper and the pedestal is made of a type of rock called granite.

NEW YORK, NEW YORK

New York City is in the state of New York. New York City has lots of nicknames. It is sometimes called 'the city that never sleeps' because it is always busy, even at night. It was really busy when we went.

WE TOOK A YELLOW CAB AND BOUGHT HOT DOGS FROM A HOT DOG CART.

BROADWAY SHOW

There are 41 Broadway theatres in New York City. Broadway theatres have more than 500 seats. We had to stop and see a musical while we were in New York. The singing and dancing was amazing.

LAKE ERIE

We made our way to Pennsylvania to visit Lake Erie. Lake Erie is a very big <u>freshwater</u> lake. The country of Canada is on the other side of the lake. We stood on the beach at the shore and enjoyed the view.

THE GREAT LAKES

Lake Erie is part of the Great Lakes. There are five Great Lakes and they are called Superior, Michigan, Huron, Ontario and Erie. Lake Superior is the biggest. There are lots of lighthouses around the lakes so we visited one.

WE CLIMBED TO THE TOP OF A LIGHTHOUSE.

LAKE ERIE WATER SNAKES

We looked out for the water snakes that live around Lake Erie. They live on the shoreline near the waters of the lake. Dad said there is a legend about an eight-metre-long snake in Lake Erie called Bessie.

I WONDER IF BESSIE IS REAL.

WILD COYOTES

As we drove through Pennsylvania, we saw coyotes in the wild. Coyotes usually live in woods, but sometimes they come into cities and towns. They are a bit like dogs and wolves.

DAD SAID THAT COYOTES CAN BE FOUND ALL OVER THE USA.

MILLENNIUM PARK

We made it to the Millennium Park in Chicago, which is in the state of Illinois. The park used to be a big railroad but it was made into a green space. There is a big pavilion where people can see concerts.

PAVILION →

CLOUD GATE

I have always wanted to see Cloud Gate. It is a big <u>sculpture</u> by a British artist called Anish Kapoor. It is made out of steel. You can see the sky and the clouds reflected when you look at it.

CLOUD GATE IS SOMETIMES CALLED THE BEAN.

FOOTBALL IN CHICAGO

American football is my favourite sport, so we stopped to watch a football game at Soldier Field Stadium. Chicago's biggest football team is called the Chicago Bears.

Go Chicago Bears!

DEEP-DISH

We had to try a famous Chicago-style, deep-dish pizza before we left. The pizza was so deep that it was a bit like a pie. It was full of sausage and cheese and it had lots of tomato sauce on top.

DEEP-DISH PIZZA WAS INVENTED BY ITALIAN-AMERICANS LIVING IN CHICAGO.

MOUNT RUSHMORE NATIONAL MEMORIAL

After a long drive, we arrived in the state of South Dakota to see Mount Rushmore. Mount Rushmore is a special landmark that has been carved into the side of a mountain in the Black Hills. We went on a tour to learn more.

GEORGE WASHINGTON

THOMAS JEFFERSON

THEODORE ROOSEVELT

ABRAHAM LINCOLN

WHO ARE THEY?

The faces that have been carved into the mountain are the faces of four presidents. They are George Washington, Thomas Jefferson, Theodore Roosevelt and Abraham Lincoln. These four presidents are very important to American history.

GUTZON BORGLUM

The faces were carved by a sculptor called Gutzon Borglum. It took him and around 400 other people 14 years to carve the faces. They used <u>dynamite</u> to remove big chunks of the mountain before they could carve into it.

THIS IS WHAT IT LOOKED LIKE WHEN WORKERS WERE CARVING LINCOLN.

HISTORY OF THE BLACK HILLS

We learnt all about the history of the Black Hills and the Sioux Nation. The Sioux Nation was made up of Native American and First Nations tribes that lived around the Black Hills. Many tribespeople lived in tepees.

TEPEE

SPACE NEEDLE

We drove to Seattle, in the state of Washington. I've always wanted to visit the Space Needle. It opened in 1962 and is a symbol of Seattle. The Space Needle is 184 metres tall.

TO THE OBSERVATION DECK

We went all the way up the Space Needle in an elevator to the observation level. The floor was made of glass. It was a bit scary because we were so high up, but I could see all of Seattle.

SPACE NEEDLE COORDINATES
47.6204743,
-122.349193

ALL ABOARD THE MONORAIL

We went on the monorail when we were in Seattle. The monorail is a train that has one train track. The track has been built above the city. When we went on the monorail, we could see everybody walking on the streets below.

THE MONORAIL WAS BUILT IN 1962.

THE SASQUATCH

Seattle is in the state of Washington, which is in an area called the Pacific Northwest. There is a legend in the Pacific Northwest about a big creature called the Sasquatch. A lot of people in Washington say they have seen the Sasquatch, so we kept a look out for it.

THE SASQUATCH IS ALSO CALLED BIGFOOT.

THE SASQUATCH HAS GIANT FEET AND LOTS OF BROWN FUR.

GOLDEN GATE BRIDGE

We left Seattle and made our way to the city of San Francisco in California. We crossed the famous Golden Gate Bridge on our way. It is huge!

The Golden Gate Bridge is 1,280 metres long and has towers that are 227 metres high. It was the longest bridge in the world when it was built in 1937. The bridge has been painted bright orange and lots of tourists come to visit and take photographs on it.

WE STOPPED NEARBY AND TOOK A PHOTO WITH THE BRIDGE!

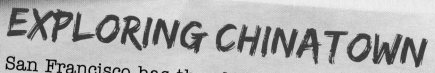

EXPLORING CHINATOWN

San Francisco has the oldest Chinatown in the USA. Workers came from China to the USA around the year 1848, and since then the Chinese <u>community</u> has grown and Chinatown has got bigger and bigger.

A LOT OF BUILDINGS ARE INSPIRED BY CHINESE ARCHITECTURE.

TIN HOW TEMPLE

We visited the Tin How Temple. It is the oldest Chinese temple in the USA. It was built in 1852. The temple is dedicated to the Chinese <u>deity</u> Mazu. Mazu protected the workers when they sailed across the sea to come to the USA.

WE ATE LOTS OF DIM SUM IN CHINATOWN TOO!

25

MESA VERDE NATIONAL PARK

The last stop on our trip was Mesa Verde National Park in Colorado. The park is Native American land. About 1,400 years ago, the <u>Ancestral Pueblo people</u> built their homes in Mesa Verde.

CLIFF DWELLINGS

There are around 600 cliff dwellings in the park. We learnt that the cliff dwellings were used by the Ancestral Pueblo people as houses. Some dwellings had rooms called kivas. Kivas were rooms used for religion.

CLIFF PALACE IS A HUGE CLIFF DWELLING WITH AROUND 170 ROOMS.

GOLDEN EAGLES

There is a lot of wildlife in the park. Mom spotted a golden eagle. It is one of the largest birds in the USA. Golden eagles have sharp talons that they use to catch their prey.

GOLDEN EAGLES EAT ANIMALS SUCH AS RABBITS, SQUIRRELS AND OTHER BIRDS.

AMERICAN BLACK BEAR

We had to watch out for black bears around Mesa Verde. Black bears eat a lot of berries and plants. They also eat fish. They can be very dangerous to humans.

THE JOURNEY

Look at the places we visited on our road trip across the USA!

MOUNT RUSHMORE NATIONAL MEMORIAL

SPACE NEEDLE

I WILL FIND YOU, SASQUATCH.

GOLDEN GATE BRIDGE

MESA VERDE NATIONAL PARK

PASSPO

MILLENNIUM PARK

LAKE ERIE

THE STATUE OF LIBERTY

THE WHITE HOUSE

WASHINGTON MONUMENT

EVERGLADES NATIONAL PARK

THE FRENCH QUARTER

I LOVE OYSTERS NOW.

HOUSTON SPACE CENTRE

GOODBYE

We didn't get to visit every state in the USA, but we still saw a lot! I loved seeing the different cultures and landmarks of each state. It's amazing how different each state is.

My favourite place to visit was the French Quarter in New Orleans. There was great architecture and I had never been to Mardi Gras before. Everything was happy and colourful. I loved all the delicious food, especially the oysters!

GLOSSARY

amendments	laws that have been added to the Constitution
Ancestral Pueblo people	a group of Native American people that lived in the US states of New Mexico, Colorado and Utah many many years ago
architecture	the design and style of a building
carnival	an occasion of celebration
community	a group of people who live and work in the same area
cuisine	a style or method of cooking often related to a particular place or country
culture	the way of life and traditions of a group of people
deity	a god or goddess
dynamite	an explosive material
exhibition	an event where objects or art are shown to the public
federal	an authority that is central to an area
floats	moving platforms with decorations, usually used in parades
freshwater	water that is not salty and doesn't come from the sea
government	the group of people who run a country and decide its laws
independence	freedom from outside control or authority
monument	a building or structure built to remember someone or something
obelisk	a tall stone structure that has four sides with a pyramid shape at the top
pedestal	a support or base for a statue or another object
replica	an exact copy or model of something
reptiles	cold-blooded animals with scales
sculpture	a three-dimensional object that has been made to be looked at
shallow	when water is not very deep

INDEX

A
alligators 11
architecture 8, 25, 30

B
bears 27
Broadway 15

C
Chinatown, the 25
climate 11
Constitution, the 5
coyotes 17

F
food
- creole 9
- dim sum 25
- hot dogs 15
- pizza 19
- Tex-Mex 7

L
legends
- Bessie 17
- Sasquatch 23, 28

M
Mardi Gras 9, 30
Mississippi River 8
mountains 20, 21

N
Native Americans 9, 21, 26-27

P
plants 11, 27

W
Washington, George 12-13, 20